Flood Warning

A play

Fay Weldon

Samuel French—London
New York-Toronto-Hollywood

©2003 BY FAY WELDON

Rights of Performance by Amateurs are controlled by Samuel French Ltd, 52 Fitzroy Street, London W1T 5JR, and they, or their authorized agents, issue licences to amateurs on payment of a fee. **It is an infringement of the Copyright to give any performance or public reading of the play before the fee has been paid and the licence issued.**

The Royalty Fee indicated below is subject to contract and subject to variation at the sole discretion of Samuel French Ltd.

    Basic fee for each and every
        performance by amateurs   Code E
        in the British Isles

The Professional Rights to this play are controlled by CASAROTTO RAMSAY AND ASSOCIATES LTD, WAVERLY HOUSE, 7-12 NOEL STREET, LONDON W1F 8GQ

The publication of this play does not imply that it is necessarily available for performance by amateurs or professionals, either in the British Isles or Overseas. Amateurs and professionals considering a production are strongly advised in their own interests to apply to the appropriate agents for written consent before starting rehearsals or booking a theatre or hall.

ISBN 978 0 573 02361 3

Please see page iv for further copyright information

FLOOD WARNING

First produced in 2002 with the following cast of characters:

Cynthia	Gillian Oxley
Step	Alan Chalcroft
Trevor	Brian Watts
Jane	Jacqueline Beatty
Angela	Denise Baldwin

The play was directed by Candice Marcus
Produced by Simon Hunt

COPYRIGHT INFORMATION
(See also page ii)

This play is fully protected under the Copyright Laws of the British Commonwealth of Nations, the United States of America and all countries of the Berne and Universal Copyright Conventions.

All rights, including Stage, Motion Picture, Radio, Television, Public Reading, and Translation into Foreign Languages, are strictly reserved.

No part of this publication may lawfully be reproduced in ANY form or by any means — photocopying, typescript, recording (including video-recording), manuscript, electronic, mechanical, or otherwise — or be transmitted or stored in a retrieval system, without prior permission.

Licences are issued subject to the understanding that it shall be made clear in all advertising matter that the audience will witness an amateur performance; that the names of the authors of the plays shall be included on all announcements and on all programmes; and that the integrity of the authors' work will be preserved.

The Royalty Fee is subject to contract and subject to variation at the sole discretion of Samuel French Ltd.

In Theatres or Halls seating Four Hundred or more the fee will be subject to negotiation.

In Territories Overseas the fee quoted in this Acting Edition may not apply. A fee will be quoted on application to our local authorized agent, or if there is no such agent, on application to Samuel French Ltd, London.

VIDEO-RECORDING OF AMATEUR PRODUCTIONS

Please note that the copyright laws governing video-recording are extremely complex and that it should not be assumed that any play may be video-recorded for *whatever purpose* without first obtaining the permission of the appropriate agents. The fact that a play is published by Samuel French Ltd does not indicate that video rights are available or that Samuel French Ltd controls such rights.

CHARACTERS

Cynthia, once an artist, now an antique dealer; late 50s
Step, her husband, ex-army, now an antique dealer; late 50s
Trevor, an unsuccessful set designer with principles, Jane's partner; 30ish
Jane, Cynthia's and Step's daughter, ambitious and forceful, a successful city broker; 35ish
Angela: her sister, quiet, domestic, plain, a primary-school-teacher; 25ish

The action takes place in a room above an antique shop in the market square of a cathedral town

Time—the present

Also by Fay Weldon, published by Samuel French Ltd

Action Replay
I Love My Love
The Reading Group (one act)

FLOOD WARNING

The living-room above a shop, which is a classy antique emporium in the market square of a cathedral town. Evening

We are in the front room, which overlooks the square, and is Step's and Cynthia's living-room: pleasant and well furnished. The sense is of old oak beams and not quite enough space for comfort. There is a door R leading to the kitchen

Cynthia sits at the window with her leg in plaster, looking out at the worrying scene outside. The door to the stairs is open, and Step and Angela can be seen moving up cardboard boxes from which they carefully unpack decanters, candlesticks, Clarice Cliff and so forth on to the landing shelves. This is a delicate rescue operation: the boxes have to be set free for the next load. Cynthia talks half to Step and Angela, half to herself

Cynthia I told them so. You're not supposed to say that, are you, "I told you so." But I did. I told the Council. I said if you build your fancy new estates down there on the water meadows the Helmer will finally break its banks and this town will flood. And what did they say, those appalling young women at the planning office, with their degrees and their little simpering self-righteous smiles, and their profound ignorance of everything that matters? They said, "Oh madam, rainfall would have to break all records before that happens." And rainfall did break all records, and now look.
Step At least you have the satisfaction of proving them right.
Cynthia Oh, were you listening? I didn't think you would be. That makes a change.
Step But I always listen to you.

Cynthia I feel sorry for the river.

Angela You what, Mother?

Cynthia Hemmed in, insulted, trapped, embanked, its mud flats gone, its water meadows nothing but a trading estate, not an eel nor an elder to its name, how else is it going to react? It's going to lash out, isn't it? Try and destroy everyone, everything. I know what it feels like. I'm on its side.

Step You're depressed because of your leg. Only another couple of days and the plaster comes off.

Cynthia How am I going to get to the hospital? In a boat? How am I going to get in the boat? I'll sink it.

Step I don't think it will come to that, sweetheart.

Cynthia Don't you? I reckon that water's already six inches deep where it's running down the middle of the road, and it's rising. Soon we won't be able to open our own front door. All those people filling sandbags — what a waste of effort. The water just took another route. I told them it would. They hated me for it. I did shout rather. It was so windy and messy and inefficient, it drove me mad. When all this is over I suppose I'll have to go round saying I'm sorry.

Step I daresay they know you well enough by now, Cynthia, to forgive you. You've been a councillor for sixteen years: they might even make you mayor, eventually. I've been one for eighteen and I'm always nice to everyone but they won't ask me. It's you they need.

Cynthia That's ridiculous. Who said that? I'm not the kind to be mayor. I'm always on the wrong side of the fence. I'm just seen as the local busybody. People throw up their hands when they see me coming and flee, I know they do.

Step Sorry, my dear, they take you seriously.

Cynthia But I don't feel like a serious person. I feel like a delinquent. That I'm going to be found out any moment, exposed as a fraud. I suppose that's the way it goes. One day the switch is thrown: you're no longer the tenant trying to pay the rent, you're the landlord trying to get it. If you're in court you're not in the dock you're on the bench. Little by little you join the forces of oppression, find yourself on the other side, turning into your own enemy. But you can never quite believe it.

Angela appears in the doorway and goes to the window to see what's happening

Angela Look at that! And it goes on raining. Forty days and forty nights — that's what it feels like, biblical. You realize we've had this place fifteen years and it's never been flooded out before? It really is climate change, isn't it? It's frightening.
Cynthia That or the new trading estate, down on the water meadows: all that concrete where it ought to be sponge. No-one's going to like me any the more because I was right, of course. God, I hate this plaster cast. Now I know what it's like to be old: every step an effort, trapped in one place, wanting to get on all the time and not able to. Are you sure everything's out of the shop? I can't even check.
Step We're doing fine. We've got most of the stock on to high ground, or at least piled on top of itself. No problem. Thank the Lord Jane and Trevor were down to lend a hand.
Angela What about me?
Cynthia Of course you, Angela. You always lend a hand. But you live here; they visit, so we notice.
Angela Jane actually has biceps. I noticed when we were moving the refectory tables up from the basement. She took off her jacket and like, wow. She's taken to going to the gym: working out and body building. I'm sure she's stronger than Trevor. Not that that's saying much. I can't talk: all I do by way of exercise is play the school piano for the Infants: plonkety-plonk. "Away in a Manger", "Summer Holiday". I was just not born to move heavy furniture the way Jane seems to be. I've got a splinter in my finger, too. Ouch!

Trevor enters from downstairs

Trevor Jane says we need to bring the St Peter up the stairs. It's a soft wood, not even painted round the base: it'll get damaged. She says for me to ask is there any space left up here? It is quite big. Is something the matter with your finger, Angel?
Angela Splinter.

During the following, Trevor goes to look at it, tries to get it out with his fingers, decides teeth would be better and tries with them

Cynthia Please not. I don't want St Peter up here. He's so censorious. That bunch of keys, barring the gate to heaven. You shouldn't have bought him, Step. He'll never sell: just hang around taking up shop space. All the other saints go like hot cakes. St Michael's always a winner, St Peter's a no-no, my father told me all that: he specialized in Church furniture. I'd leave St Peter to take his chances, hope to God he floats away down the street and we can claim on the insurance.

Step That seems a bit drastic, love. Let St Peter come up. He'll just about fit. I like him. A very fine piece of carving.

Cynthia You did post off the premium?

Step Of course. I take it rather badly that you should ask.

Cynthia Sorry. You know how forgetful you can be.

Step Not about things like that.

Trevor manages to get the splinter out

Angela Thank you, Trevor. No-one else cared. I think that's really delinquent of you, Mum, to want to leave St Peter to his fate. Supposing someone found out?

Trevor If Jane says move St Peter, we'd better move St Peter. Saves time and energy in the end, to do as she says at the beginning.

Cynthia I thought you and she were going to try for the 6.40 back to London.

Trevor The road's flooded and the station's closed. Bloody nuisance. Jane says we'll stay overnight and help out, if that's OK with you, and make our escape first thing tomorrow.

Cynthia Where are you going to sleep? The spare room's so full of stock you won't be able to get to the bed.

Angela Jane will manage.

Trevor We can't leave you three in the lurch.

Angela But Trevor, you said you had an important meeting tomorrow morning, what about that?

Trevor Well, it could have turned out to be important. Just my luck that it won't happen. A new contact I made. He's flying back to Hollywood tomorrow night. A big budget film too, not even art house, special effects but minimalist, just up my street. Too bad. Fate sends flood as punishment for our sins.

Angela What sin?

Trevor The being out of work sin.

Cynthia The new estate on the water meadows sin, if you ask me.

Step We're all so guilty. I should have reminded you to do up your shoelaces, Cynthia, so you didn't trip and fall, which you did, breaking your leg. God knows I feel remorseful.

Cynthia That was a misdemeanour, not a sin. I'd only have shouted and said don't come between me and my laces, my shoes are my business.

Step That's what I thought. That's why I stayed quiet.

Angela I take it Jane has nothing in particular on tomorrow?

Trevor No, as it happens. Anyway she's such a big cheese these days people re-arrange themselves around her.

Angela Or it might be politically expedient for her to be not at her desk in the morning, something like that.

Trevor Well yes, I daresay ——

Angela Because frankly I can't believe my sister Jane would let a small thing like a flood and a closed station keep her away from the office unless it suited her. She'd call a helicopter. What is more she'd be able to afford one. How come I always do the right thing and live on a public servant's pay and she works for global corporations and can afford helicopters? What is the difference between us?

Cynthia opens her mouth to say something, glances at Step and closes it again

Step Luck of the genes, my dear.

Angela Unluck, more like it.

Jane (*off*) Please, somebody, anybody, what about St Peter? We need to get a move on. There's a flood out there and it's rising, and I can see the water coming under the front door. Only a trickle, but many a trickle makes a muckle, or something. I'm going to get my boots wet and they're Gucci! Trevor!

Trevor Sorry, darling.

Trevor jumps to it and exits downstairs

Angela sighs

Step At least, if we're going to be trapped, we're all together as a family. Mind you, if it was just you and me, Cynthia, how romantic it would be. But there you are, we had the girls.

Angela Thank you very much. I'm sorry if I'm in the way. Did you actually want me, or was I an accident? I've always felt kind of accidental.

Cynthia Pass.

Angela Dad?

Step Pass.

Angela So I was an accident. Was Jane? Bet she wasn't ...

Cynthia Pass.

Step I'll see if there's any beer left in the fridge, though I have a feeling Trevor finished it all last night. I did ask you to get in emergency supplies, Angela, when we got the first flood warnings, and what you got in was extra candles and tuna — thank you very much — but no extra beer. I don't understand young women.

Step goes out to the kitchen

Angela All I ever get is criticism. It is very bad for my self-esteem. Doesn't he realize that? I could probably sue under the Human Rights Act for bad fathering.

Cynthia Angela, give over. Just allow things to be as they are. You've been so fidgety lately. The flood is rising, the water's under the door, this town is officially marooned, trade will fall off, the business is going to go bankrupt, your father and I will be left with nothing, I've broken my leg — and you're talking about suing your father?

Angela I was only joking, Mum. A homeopathic dose of misery. My own little bit of tragedy. I do have some to offer, you'd be surprised.

Cynthia So you're young, so you've no idea the kind of thing that can happen next.

Angela Oh, I have, believe me. But you're the one who needs to cheer up. So what's new? You've been on the edge of bankruptcy since forever, but we still seem to live here and have shoes on our feet and food on the table, and every now and then Dad sells something, if only by accident.

Jane (*off*) Trev, for heaven's sake, steer to the right not the left, and then you'll be over the ledge. I thought men were meant to be more spatially aware than women. Angela, stop sulking and come and help, this is impossible. Daddy, whatever you're doing, please stop it and come and help.

A bang and a crash and a shriek or two from downstairs

Jane appears, brash and beautiful and full of a supreme and careless self-confidence

Now I can't get down and Trevor can't get up. St Peter is wedged. At least I was on the right side when disaster happened. Trevor has only the watery ground, but the sky is mine. That figures. Those keys of St Peter's aren't original. They're metal. They jangle. I hope Daddy didn't pay too much for him. Where is Daddy?

Angela In the kitchen looking for beer.

Jane Look at that rain! It's Sodom and Gomorrah, punishment for our sins.

Angela Sodom and Gomorrah was salt, not water.

Jane You're so clever at Bible-y things, Angela. You always went to Sunday school — I never did. Couldn't you come and help with St Peter? Trevor has to be rescued. You'd be good at that.

Angela St Peter was perfectly OK where he was. It wouldn't have harmed him to get his feet wet.

Jane Oh, happy holidays. Happy weekend in the country.

Jane goes downstairs again. Step returns from the kitchen

Step No beer.

Angela Sorry.

Step Still, we have a lot to be thankful for.

Cynthia What? For example?

Step We could be running a delicatessen not an antiques shop. When I came out of the army it was on the cards. But we chose right. Unlike cheese, antiques have the opposite of a sell-by date. The older the better, the higher the price, and a bit of damp doesn't make much difference.

Cynthia Not much of a decision. I hate olives and I come from a long line of antique dealers. And all you knew was about tanks. But you soon learned. Now people prefer buying from you than from me. They catch your enthusiasm. All they get from me is doubt and that's bad for business. There's a kind of tidal wave coming: up from the Market Square. Bits of wood and a bicycle and lots of paper and gunge. This is getting really bad. If they have any sense they'll dynamite half a mile up just before the Eely runs into the Helmer. Divert the flow. The water will be through the bank's windows soon. They hardly moved a thing out before they left: all their computers are still in there. Do you think they'll lose our files?

Angela No such luck. I expect they keep them centrally, on disk.

Cynthia Well, we can always hope. I'm trying to stay cheerful. I can't keep it up for long. Do you realize how bad for business this is going to be, Step? You're so optimistic: you think rain stops, and the flood recedes and the sun comes out and everything's back to normal but it's not going to be like that. Do you know what it's like, the smell of flood in a house, especially an old house like this one? How every scrap of carpet has to come out, how the wood goes rotten behind the skirtings? How there's more sewage in the world than anyone realizes? Do you realize?

Step My dear, we have been married for most of our adult lives. My life experience is pretty much the same as yours: so yes, I do know. It is just in my nature to look on the bright side. The flood will subside, the sun will indeed come out, the tourists will return, the price of antiques will rise slowly but surely over the years. As supply dries up, demand rises. You can't lose with antiques. Have some faith. There might be some beer Trevor missed in the top cupboard.

Step goes back into the kitchen

Cynthia (*after him*) How are we going to pay the tax bill in January? Income will drop, there'll be nothing for new stock. We're scraping by as it is, since the Foot and Mouth, since the Twin Towers, since the tourists left. What kind of world are we living in? Perpetual anxiety: about money, about family; open the papers and it's all sudden disaster, and now even nature seems to be against us. We've worked hard all our lives, we should be living in peace and comfort, and what I have we got? This. Flood water rising, the past adding up to nothing, and as for the future — there isn't any. Where are my grandchildren? I have two daughters. Jane apparently can't. Angela simply won't.

Angela Oh dear, dead-branch-on-the-tree-of-life stuff again. It's not that way round, Mum. It's Jane who won't. She's the one with the home, the permanent partner, the income and the energy. Just no window in her diary for babies. If it was me I'd throw the diary away. But it isn't me. And I'm not like her. I believe babies should be born into proper homes to properly partnered couples or forget it. And I don't have a man or a home so how do I get to have a baby?

Cynthia You're too picky. As soon as a man steps over the door you send him away. Too brash, or too dull, or you'd rather go out with your girlfriends.

Step comes in from the kitchen holding two cans of beer

Step I found two cans. Triumph.

Angela I want true love. I have a right to true love. Everyone does. I'll wait until he comes along, thank you very much. And if he doesn't come along I've got my friends, and my career, and my freedom. Men are optional extras these days. So are babies. But I hope it happens for me. Isn't that enough for you?

Cynthia One day my prince will come. Bunkum.

Step My, you are depressed. I turned up for you, didn't I? I came along.

Cynthia Our generation was different. We were grateful for what we could get. Our children want the moon. And I am not depressed. Stop diminishing me, Step. Reducing me to a counsellor's handbook. This is the real me you're seeing and hearing, just rather more focused than usual because I can't run round doing things. I'm trapped, so I have to sit and think. If we don't have grandchildren, if the line just stops here, what is the point of our being alive?

Step To enjoy the consumer paradise, I suppose. That seems to be the consensus. Can we postpone the soul searching till the floodwaters abate? They're so distracting.

Cynthia They'll never abate, Step, that's the point. There's always something. You and me, we stagger from one disaster to the next.

Step You'd make a lovely painting, sitting there like that. Woman in window with leg in plaster staring at flood. You are so beautiful.

More bangs and crashes from the stairwell, and swearing from Trevor

Cynthia If only I'd listened and done up my shoelaces, it could just be woman in window staring at flood.

Step Worse than the girls. I kept telling you to do double knots.

Cynthia But one likes to defy fate. I'm sorry, darling.

Angela You two love each other, why shouldn't the same happen for me?

Cynthia Because you have to be spectacularly lucky.

Jane returns

Jane Dad, you really have to come and help, because Trevor's trapped again, his own stupid fault, and the water's already up to the first stair, and he'll ruin his shoes. They're Gucci. I paid for them.

Step (*going*) OK, OK, the Gucci's must be saved, whatever they are.

Step and Jane go downstairs

Angela I could ask and ask and he wouldn't even hear me. But he does what Jane says. It isn't fair …

Cynthia You've been sniping at Jane all day. It isn't like you.

Angela Sorry. Sibling rivalry, I guess. She's got everything and I've got nothing. That old stuff. It's my own fault. Why should I bother to aspire?

Cynthia You're sweet and good and what you need is a baby.

Angela I see. I'm to have one on my own, am I? From a sperm bank, perhaps? On the salary of an infant school teacher? You're joking.

Cynthia God, your generation is so mercenary. Can't you ever hold your noses and just jump?

Angela You say I'm too picky but I'm not. Chance would be a fine thing. I'm not Jane. Men crowd round her like wasps round the honey, but they just look through me and past me, or else they want me for a bit of rest and recreation, when bruised from the fray with her. And then they leave me. And that is the true story of my life, not the picky, principled rejecter of suitors. Why do I have to be so different from her? It isn't fair.

A bang and a crash

Jane lopes in

Jane That's OK then. Dad can get a job as a removal man if this finally all goes wrong. St Peter is tucked away on the landing, out of harm's way. Make us some tea, Angela, there's a love. I'm whacked.

Angela (*meekly*) Ordinary breakfast or that green stuff?

Jane The green. It's what keeps the Japanese healthy.

Angela goes off into the kitchen

Cynthia I don't know how you and Trevor can drink that stuff. It's so peculiar.

Jane That's why you live in the country, not the city. You're averse to change. God knows which comes first. No green tea and the country, or the country and no green tea. And what's the matter with my sister? She won't look me in the eye and she keeps sniping. Have I done something?

Cynthia You exist. That's enough. Sibling envy.
Jane Time she found a boyfriend.
Cynthia I brought you two girls up as feminists. There's more to life than men.
Jane Only if you've got one. I worry about her. Stuck away here, still living at home, wasting her life. She's got no ambition. Shouldn't she be on anti-depressants or something?
Cynthia She's happy enough with a quiet life. She loves her job, teaching little children too small to answer back. She sings in the local choir: they're all going up to the Albert Hall for a concert, that's quite an event round here. I know it all sounds like hell to you. I can see it must be a great trial, you and Trevor having to stay a day later than planned.
Jane Trevor seemed to actually want to come, this time. I didn't have to drag him. And you're my mum and dad, and I have to make sure you're all right from time to time. I do sometimes wish you'd arranged your lives better, so you were more like other people's parents, and had parquet floors and lived down a country lane with proper pensions, not trying to keep a failing antiques business on the road.
Cynthia It is not failing; it is going through a bad patch. You can't lose out on antiques. Your father says so.

Jane is looking out the window, not listening

Jane The flow's changed again. It's coming down between the bank and the estate agents. And is that Dad's old Volvo up in the parking lot? It keeps rising off its wheels and then plonking down again. I don't believe this. It's going to take off on its own any minute. Why didn't he drive it to higher ground?
Cynthia He didn't think it would be as bad as this. Nobody did.
Jane If Dad didn't send off the insurance money I don't want you to worry. I got a stupendous bonus this year: I'll see you right, Mum. I'll pay for cleaning up and redecorating, all that stuff. And you can have my car: it's time I got a new one. Once all this is over. When the town is back to being a town, and the roads stop being rivers. But he will have sent it. Won't he?

Flood Warning 13

Cynthia It said on the radio they're going to blow up the banks upstream, in order to ease the situation. A sort of large scale, last resort plumbing. Then the batteries went dead — as they do.

Jane Only in this house.

Cynthia If you wanted a baby nothing would stop you. But you don't want one.

Jane Please don't start that again or I'll go back to London even if I have to swim. And you only want grandchildren because you're bored, so please shut up about it. You're putting a guilt trip on me. It isn't fair.

Cynthia I'm sure Trevor would love to be a father. He's such a nice responsible man.

Jane Perhaps you're the one who should feel guilty. You don't care about me, only about a possible baby. What about my figure, what about my wealth, and my nerves, and my spare time, and my holidays? I would be a rotten mother. But you don't care. All you want me for is breeding stock.

Cynthia Jane, I don't think you are happy.

Jane What an extraordinary thing to say. I have a lovely flat, a lovely man, friends, holidays, a glorious career: no spare time for brooding. I even love my mother and father and my sister, though that may surprise you. Yes, I think that adds up to happiness.

Cynthia But do you love Trevor?

Jane I get on with him, we share interests. It's not passion, I don't adore him, if that's what you mean, the way you do Dad. I could only admire someone who's my superior and where am I going to find someone better than me? I like going to bed with him.

Cynthia Then why don't you want his child?

Jane Because there's more to life than just handing it on. I just don't feel like swelling up and podding off, somehow. It so animal. Yuk.

Cynthia All our forebears going back into history — making such sacrifices, giving up their own lives — and then it's all just to stop ...

Jane Perhaps we've gone as far we need. Sure, our line of descent will die out, if Angela and I don't oblige, but there's enough people left in the world to be getting on with.

Angela comes back in with a tray of tea which she hands out during the following

Angela Jane, I have something to tell you. I have to, because not is making me bad tempered and that's bad for me. And honesty is so important, isn't it?

Jane It never seemed to me honesty was in the least important. In my experience people only tell you the truth when they want to hurt you.

Angela But it concerns you very profoundly, Jane. And, Mum, you need to know too. I need you to be there for me. I thought I could manage but I'm hurting so badly inside.

Jane Oh dear, dear and that can give you cancer. You are such an attention seeker, Angela. I'm having a nice talk with Mum and nothing will do but you have to break it up. Couldn't you just get a life?

Angela Please stop her being so horrid to me, Mum. I'm not up to it. I'm really low. I've been and gone and got pregnant. And now I feel sick and so funny in the head, I need you, Mum.

Cynthia Angel — you're having a baby! but that is totally wonderful!

Jane There you are, Mum. Problem solved. Big sister let off hook. Thank you, Angie. You are a dark horse. Whose is it? Dad's?

Angela Don't be so totally disgusting.

Jane It's just you don't seem to get out much. One's bound to wonder. And not much hanky-panky on the coach to the Albert Hall, I imagine.

Angela Whose it is is totally irrelevant. I'm not going through with it, I can't, because there isn't a proper father. Not one who'll stay with me and help. He would if he could, but he can't because he's with somebody else. So I'm not going through with it. I'm having a termination, I have no option.

Jane Then why the fuss? Why even mention it?

Cynthia Angela, let's talk about this. You mustn't do anything too quickly.

Angela I was going down to the clinic today, I had an appointment, but I can't keep it because of the flood. I feel so sick and peculiar.

Cynthia You'll get over that. That passes. Thank God for the flood. You'll regret it all your life if you terminate. Have the baby; if you can't manage, don't want it, then give it to me.

Angela But that wouldn't be fair on the baby. Every baby deserves a mother's love.

Jane That's daft. Most people would rather be alive than not have been born at all, just because their background didn't come up to social welfare specifications. If it's a question of money, I'll do the supporting, just so long as no-one wants me to wipe its butt. I don't mind babies in principle; it's just the detail is so appalling. What I need to know if I'm going to pay is who the father is? Black, white, in between? What sort of genes are involved? Are we talking organ master or passing homeless? Some illegal immigrant looking for a passport? What are we getting here?

Angela You are so totally trivial, Jane. It's Trevor's.

Silence

Jane (*finally*) No come now, that's not possible.

Angela I didn't mean to tell you. It just came out.

Jane Bet it did. It hasn't been unknown to.

Angela You make me so angry. Just because you're so wonderful doesn't mean I'm the opposite. I am not exactly deformed; your legs are longer, and you pass exams and make money, but that doesn't mean I'm the pits. I'm sure I'm a lot nicer than you are.

Jane You're trying to upset me. It can't possibly be Trevor. You're hardly his type, and anyway the sister-in-law thing would turn him right off. So Jerry Springer. And anyway he'd have told me.

Angela He doesn't know. I didn't tell him. He'd only have told you. I didn't want to upset you, because I do love you even though you're so foul. You're my sister. I'm so sorry. I want you to know that we were really careful, we talked about you a lot. You were there with us. He wore a thing but it broke.

Jane Thank you so much for sharing that with me, Angela.

Cynthia I forbid you to do away with this child. It's murder.

Angela It was back in the summer, one weekend, probably last time you were home, Jane, and you and Mum and Dad had gone to the cinema and I was stock-taking and Trevor had seen the film and he was feeling really low. You don't love him, Jane; you just need him to boss around. He's like me, he feels he can never do anything right. He's like a shadow of you, the way I am, two shadows of you, finally getting together. And I kissed him I was so sorry for him and one thing led to another, just a sort of stupid grapple on the sofa, we agreed not to talk about it, it was over before it began, never to mention it, for everyone's sake, but then I got pregnant. It is so horrible. You have this thing growing inside you like a kind of growth, there's no stopping it ——

Jane is at the door

Jane (*shouting down the stairs*) Trevor!
Cynthia It's not a thing, it's a child. My grandchild
Angela Oh God, I shouldn't have said anything, I knew I shouldn't.

Trevor comes running, followed by Step

Trevor What is it? What's the matter?
Jane Were you and my sister lovers?
Trevor (*to Angela*) You didn't go and tell ——
Angela I'm sorry, it was too much of a secret — like porridge overflowing when you make it in the microwave — there was no stopping it.
Jane Were you two lovers?
Step What's going on? It's never advisable to make porridge in a microwave.
Jane Happy families is going on.
Trevor Angela, we had a pact not to mention it.
Angela But I got pregnant. No, we, you're part of it. You and me and pregnant. Don't worry about it. I had an appointment at the clinic today. A termination.
Trevor You can't do that. Without consultation.

Jane You're out, Trevor. That's the end. With my own sister. I'm not speaking to you again. You've holed your own boat. You're sunk. (*To Cynthia and Step*) And if you two harbour this criminal, this horrible accident, that's the last you see of me, too. I hope that's clear. (*To Angela*) Your revenge on me, I suppose. For being born plain, dumb, pompous and second.

Step Now Jane, if you can't say anything nice don't say anything at all.

Jane My little sister. She was always trying to steal my toys. She was so sneaky. She'd choose her time and let out a scream and then you'd think I'd done something to hurt her, and I'd be the one to get told off.

Angela Don't let her hurt you, Trevor. You see how she thinks of you? A toy. Something to be broken and replaced? She is so shallow.

Jane Termination is the only answer. It is not fair to the world to let her genes loose on it. The wheel may go on turning but the hamster's died. And Trevor's not much better. A sandwich short of a filling.

Trevor Jane, don't say things you'll regret later. You're upset now, I understand that. But you were the one who wanted an open relationship. It's a two-way street. I was upset about you and that Patel millionaire fellow. Jealous, even. I knew it was only for the money and the investment opportunities, but even so, it hurt. I know it was a breach of loyalty ——

Step My God, how the young live.

Cynthia It was meant. She has to have the baby.

Trevor (*to Jane*) And Angela is a darling, gentle and loving. You are very hard on her.

Jane I can see you might suit each other very well. Two failures, two ineffectual hangers-on, Angela still living at home, you unemployed, living off me — why don't you just stay, move in, share her room, get back under the parental eye. Live here in this dump, infantilized, maximalist hell instead of minimalist heaven. Not even a power shower. Unironed shirts. Nowhere to hang your ties.

Cynthia There would just about be space here — now that could be managed ——

Step Don't interfere with their lives, Cynthia. If we want this to be the sort of thing that blows over, fades into the past, just a rather nasty family row to be forgotten as soon as possible ——

Jane (*rounding on her father*) Fade into the past! This? I cannot believe you're my father. You are so crap. I just don't understand your mentality. Can't you defend me? Have you no anger in you? Daddy, please be on my side. Throw him out!

Cynthia Angela, don't throw away God's gift to you.

Angela But I can't afford it.

Step What do you want me to do? Put Trevor out to be drowned?

Jane Poor Trevor! What about poor me?

Angela He's your partner, Jane, you can't throw him out, just like that.

Jane I don't see why not. He has no rights under the law. He came freely, he goes freely. No high-earning woman should ever get married. Men cannot help being bastards.

Step I can only conclude I'm not a man.

Jane You're not man enough to be a bastard. You're excused. But this just-about male personage, this sneaky wimp, this Trevor, most certainly is: he has betrayed me, seduced Angela, my virgin sister, invaded her body space and made her pregnant ——

Angela I was not so a virgin. And I did most of the seducing — you have to with New Men, and that's what you turned him into. A house husband without even a child to look after. I am so sorry for Trevor, being with you. You have drained all the substance out of him. He is your fault.

Step Shouldn't we all just be quiet, so that no-one says anything they might regret. Let's look at this coolly: Angela has been made pregnant by Trevor, who is her elder sister's partner. This is not such a rare or extraordinary event. It happens on Kilroy Silk all the time.

Jane How come you're my father?

Step I get tired of you saying that. I'd pick you up at the school gate and I was never good enough for you. There was always a younger looking man with more hair and better teeth and a new car you wished was the one to collect you.

Jane I don't remember doing that. Did I do that? What a little brat! I'm sorry.
Step And the thing is, I was not your father. Never was your father.

A silence

Cynthia You know that?
Step Yes.
Cynthia How long have you known it?
Step From the beginning.
Cynthia Why didn't you tell me?
Step You didn't want to tell me so I thought I had better not know.
Cynthia I'm sorry. I didn't want to hurt you.
Jane What about me? What about me? How dare you do this to me! You can't just tell me this now. When I'm reeling already. While my sister who's meant to love me has stolen the baby that's rightfully mine.
Trevor What are you talking about? Rightfully yours? You didn't want a baby. You'd never even marry me. I have rights too, and free will. You forget that. You should not have taken me for granted
Jane Be quiet, Trevor. Who was my father, then?
Cynthia I have no idea.
Jane You slut!
Step Yes, who was he, as a matter of interest? Cynthia? Was it that night at the hunt ball?
Cynthia Yes, darling, it was. (*To the girls*) It was before we were married. It was one of the guests. He was young and handsome and very well spoken, that's all I can remember. So attractive and commanding I didn't stand a hope. I'd just got engaged to your father: he was playing trumpet in the army band, a boy musician. They'd go out on gigs and this time they were allowed to take wives and girlfriends. I was really thrilled. He was front line, playing trumpet. He was so talented. He looked so handsome in his red uniform. It had rows of brass buttons: a bit ridiculous I suppose, but I loved it. The only thing was they expected us to eat in the kitchen with the servants. I didn't like that. So I went

upstairs and drank all the champagne I could find just to serve them right. And there was a lot about, I can tell you. And I went off into one of the bedrooms with this young man. I am so sorry, Step. But he was drop-dead gorgeous. And I could hear you playing 'Maid of Tralee' downstairs. And honestly that's all I can remember, and you had to go back to barracks, then I was pregnant and I didn't want an abortion so I went ahead and didn't tell you it was not yours.

Step I could work out dates as well as the next man.
Cynthia I really loved you. I didn't want to upset you.
Step I knew you loved me. I saw it as just something that happened.
Jane That is disgraceful.
Cynthia What, would you rather I'd aborted you?
Angela Don't call it that. It's called a termination, I don't approve of abortions. I love little children, that's why I teach primary school.
Cynthia I would think about that then, if I were you, in your circumstances.
Jane And all this time — is that why you never loved me?
Trevor To be loved you have to be loveable. Perhaps now you'll have to try.
Jane Family is meant to love you no matter what.
Angela You know what they say, Jane? The children of lovers are orphans. That's you and me. They never had much time for either of us, only each other.
Jane Don't you-and-me me. There is no us. You slept with my boyfriend and that means you're worthless. You take after our mother. Anyone can have you …
Angela At least I'm only a half-sister. You see, there are advantages.
Jane But I want you to be my sister. I am so upset. I don't even belong in this family.
Angela That was what you always wanted. You kept telling me when I was little you'd been swapped in the hospital by mistake. You were really a princess.
Jane (*to Cynthia*) You should have told me: you're meant to tell children that kind of thing when they're small. Don't you know anything?

Flood Warning 21

Cynthia I didn't want this sort of scene. I've been putting it off for thirty-five years. (*To Step*) You should have told me you knew. All the times I had to bite my lip! It was so obvious Jane was the child of some upper-class bully — she had so much confidence — and then Angela was born so different, always trying to please, from the obsequious classes — and I couldn't even remark upon it. And I always so nervous: supposing someone had seen us that night, supposing some poison pen letter came; the longer I left it the worse it got. And I was suffering all this for you, Step, and you didn't even know it.

Jane I can't believe it. You don't even remember who my father was, you were so drunk.

Cynthia I'd never had champagne before.

Step She was very young.

Trevor This is an eye-opener. You worry far more about being illegitimate than you do about losing me, Jane. I'm just another piece of décor, an accessory in your life, a man to drape over your arm. You don't love me at all. At least Angel knows I'm real, that I think and feel and hurt.

Jane What is love, anway? Neurotic dependency. Look what it's done to my mother and the man I used to call my father. (*Wailing*) Oh, Daddy!

Step I'm still here, Jane. I'm still the same person. Nothing has changed. Please can we have less of the dramatics?

Angela There's no way I can do away with this baby: I so hate the thought of abortion. How do people do that horrible thing? It's so anti-life ... Mum, will you help me, look after it, feed it, change it, that kind of thing?

Trevor No, that's the father's job. My job. Angela?

The sound of an explosion. The Lights go off. Now they're in the dark. Trevor finds candles and matches during the following

Jane Where are the candles, for God's sake? I suppose somebody did remember — this is the absolute fucking end ——

Step That must be them blasting their way to the other river. Got a power line doing it. As you do ——

Cynthia I told them they'd have to be careful. I knew they'd make a mess of it.

Trevor lights the candles

Trevor And God said let there be light.
Angela The flood was fate, wasn't it? Destiny's way of saving the baby. I'd have been up at the clinic —I can't even bear to think of it. What a wicked person I so nearly was.
Cynthia I think the rain's stopped. And look, there's the moon. My God, things are getting better. Step, couldn't you get a hacksaw and just take this bloody cast off for me? What can they do up the hospital that you can't?
Step I'm terrible at DIY. I'd rather not, Cynthia.
Trevor I could give it a go. I'm good with my hands. I could move in here and make myself useful. Help in the shop. I did a degree in History of Art: we could specialize in paintings. There's money in that. Get the business out of the red. Marry your daughter. We all need permanence and security.
Step I'll get the hacksaw. Trevor is welcome.

Step goes

Jane What about me? Everyone's forgotten me. Just like that ...
Angela But I don't love you, Trevor. I'd have to give up my dreams to marry you, forget my hope of perfect love. Be like Jane. That's so, like, hard, when it comes to it.
Cynthia All babies mean sacrifice.
Jane Oh, really? What did you give up for me?
Cynthia I gave up the pleasure of telling the truth, Jane, on your account.
Jane (*getting out her mobile phone*) Oh that's a really good one. Blame the victim for the crime. (*She's on her mobile phone*)
Step Who are you calling? Please don't make more trouble than you have already.
Jane Me! A private detective. Who else? I have to find my father. A hunt ball nine months before I was born, an army band doing

the music, it shouldn't be too difficult getting a guest list, then it's DNA and elimination. But there's no signal. How did I come to be born to parents who are prepared to live in a town with no reliable signal?

Angela Well you weren't, were you. Sorry, I shouldn't have said that. I know you're upset. Highly strung. I'm much more placid. I think this baby is very lucky, not having you for a mother.

Jane Oh, have it your own way.

Step comes back with the hacksaw

Trevor takes it, and contemplates Cynthia's plaster cast

Trevor Which way would one cut it — horizontally or vertically?

Cynthia Look, Step, the water's going down. It's running backwards, as if the tide had turned, like water draining from a bathtub.

All run to see

Step Look what it's leaving behind. That's really nasty. You were quite right Cynthia. We'll clean it up. We'll get on our feet again, with Trevor here to help.

Trevor begins to saw away patiently

Jane Why does nobody ever take me seriously? I'm out of here. Angel, will you lend me your trainers. I'm going to walk to the station and wait for the next train. I need to be alone and think.

Step I'll give you a lift, sweetheart.

Cynthia Step, the car went with the tide. It may be days before we get it back and God knows what it will be like when we do. I haven't liked to ask, but did you actually remember to send off the insurance?

Step shakes his head. No

Cynthia I'd more or less guessed. Oh my God!

Jane Don't worry about it. My offer still stands. I'll be even richer than I was, now I won't have to house and clothe Trevor. You wore the same shirt two days running last week, Trevor. That's a sure sign of depression. I wasn't making you happy. It was time we split, anyway. I can't stand depressed men. I wasn't making you happy, I have to face it. I'll only pay for half the Volvo: the rest is damages. I'm fining Dad for his incompetence, look at it that way. People have to face the consequences of their actions.
Angela I'm going to be a mother.
Jane I'm going to be an aunt.
Angela Half-aunt.
Jane Three quarters of an aunt because the father used to be my partner.
Angela Oh all right, I'll meet you halfway.
Cynthia I did give you life, Jane. Try and be grateful.
Jane I daresay in the light of your own nature, you did your best.
Angela But will you be OK, Jane? It's all been so fast —now I've got everything and you've got nothing.
Jane You'll never manage to get St Peter back down without me. You're all such incompetents — and I'm not speaking to you, Trev, I'm not, ever again.
Trevor You will. It's not as if you really liked sex, anyway, not like Angela. It's something in your heredity, I expect. Not your fault. Just one of those things. Forget it.
Angela I wonder if there are vitamin pills in the kitchen? I really have to look after myself.

The Lights come back up again. Step blows out the candles

Angela goes out to the kitchen

Step That was quick. Everything back to normal ...

Cynthia's plaster cast falls in two. She stands and stretches. She walks a step or two

Cynthia It works! A bit stiff and tender but OK. Thanks, Trevor. Angel, where are you? When exactly is this baby to be born? We have to make plans.

Cynthia goes through to the kitchen to find Angela

Jane OK, men, let's get St Peter down while the going's good. Then I'm off.

Step, Trevor and Jane go down the stairs

The room is empty

CURTAIN

FURNITURE AND PROPERTY LIST

Only essential items are listed. Further dressing may be added at the director's discretion

On stage: Chairs
Sofa
Table
Candles and box of matches
Shelves visible on landing
Cardboard boxes containing various decanters, candlesticks, etc. visible on landing

Off stage: 2 cans of beer (**Step**)
3 cups/mugs of tea on tray (**Angela**)
Hacksaw (**Step**)

Personal: **Cynthia**: plaster cast on leg
Jane: mobile phone

LIGHTING PLOT

Practical fittings required: table lamps
Interior. The same scene throughout

To open: Full general lighting; practicals on; evening effect on window backing

Cue 1	Explosion *Black-out*	(Page 21)
Cue 2	**Trevor** lights candles *Covering light for candles*	(Page 21)
Cue 3	**Angela**: "... have to look after myself." *Snap on full general lighting and practicals*	(Page 24)

EFFECTS PLOT

Cue 1   **Trevor**: " ... My job. Angela?"   (Page 21)
Explosion

www.ingramcontent.com/pod-product-compliance
Lightning Source LLC
Chambersburg PA
CBHW070454050426
42450CB00012B/3275